U.S. ENVIRONMENTAL PROTECTION AGENCY

OFFICE OF INSPECTOR GENERAL

Review of Hotline Complaint Concerning Cost and Benefit Estimates for EPA's Lead-Based Paint Rule

Report No. 12-P-0600 July 25, 2012

Scan this mobile
code to learn more
about the EPA OIG.

Report Contributors:
Carolyn Copper
Patrick Milligan
Anne Bavuso
Kate Kimmel

Abbreviations

CASAC	Clean Air Scientific Advisory Committee
EPA	U.S. Environmental Protection Agency
IQ	Intelligence Quotient
OIG	Office of Inspector General
OMB	Office of Management and Budget
RRP	Renovation, Repair, and Paint
TSCA	Toxic Substances Control Act

Hotline

To report fraud, waste, or abuse, contact us through one of the following methods:

e-mail:	OIG_Hotline@epa.gov	**write:**	EPA Inspector General Hotline
phone:	1-888-546-8740		1200 Pennsylvania Avenue NW
fax:	202-566-2599		Mailcode 2431T
online:	http://www.epa.gov/oig/hotline.htm		Washington, DC 20460

At a Glance

Why We Did This Review

The Office of Inspector General received a hotline complaint concerning the U.S. Environmental Protection Agency's (EPA's) 2008 Lead; Renovation, Repair, and Painting Rule (Lead Rule). We conducted this review to evaluate how EPA determined the costs and benefits of the Lead Rule.

Background

The purpose of the Lead Rule was to address lead-based paint hazards created by renovation, repair, and painting activities that disturb lead-based paint in target housing. Under the rule, regulated businesses that perform renovation, repair, or painting activities must obtain EPA certification and training, and ensure that lead-safe work practices are used for projects that disturb lead-based paint. Federal agencies are required to analyze the costs and benefits of significant regulatory actions.

For further information, contact our Office of Congressional and Public Affairs at (202) 566-2391.

The full report is at:
www.epa.gov/oig/reports/2012/
20120725-12-P-0600.pdf

Review of Hotline Complaint Concerning Cost and Benefit Estimates for EPA's Lead-Based Paint Rule

What We Found

Although EPA stated that its economic analysis underwent extensive intra-Agency review and was approved by the Office of Management Budget prior to publication, EPA used limited data to develop its cost and benefit estimates for the Lead Rule. We did not conclude that EPA violated policies or failed to follow requirements in conducting its analysis. Rather, EPA conducted its economic analysis under time pressures and subsequently used its discretion to complete its analysis using some limited data and approaches. EPA's economic analyses were limited in that:

- The estimated cleaning and containment work practice costs to comply with the rule were not based on a statistically valid survey.
- EPA did not quantitatively analyze or include other costs outlined in Agency guidance, such as costs due to increased consumer prices, costs of unemployment, and costs to markets indirectly affected by the rule.
- EPA did not include the cost to renovation businesses of securing additional liability insurance.
- EPA recommended additional work practices in a training program that, while not required by the rule, would likely result in additional cost because the regulated community would view these practices as required.

Further, an EPA science advisory committee reported that limitations in the Agency's data for estimating intelligence quotient changes in children exposed to lead dust during renovations would not adequately support a rigorous cost benefit analysis. In our opinion, the data limitations in EPA's analyses limit the reliability of the rule's stated cost and benefits. In public rulemaking documents, EPA acknowledged several of the limitations. EPA's obligation under terms of a settlement agreement to issue the Lead Rule by March 2008, the use of discretion in conducting the economic analysis, and EPA's subsequent assumption that the costs of the rule were low limited EPA's approach in estimating the cost and benefits of the rule.

Recommendations/Agency Corrective Actions

We recommend that EPA reexamine the costs and benefits of the 2008 Lead Rule and the 2010 amendment to determine whether the rule should be modified, streamlined, expanded, or repealed. We also recommend that EPA add a disclaimer to its training program materials to communicate the differences between required and recommended work practices. In its response to the draft report, EPA disagreed with the first recommendation. EPA agreed with the second recommendation to clarify required work practices and made revisions.

UNITED STATES ENVIRONMENTAL PROTECTION AGENCY
WASHINGTON, D.C. 20460

July 25, 2012

MEMORANDUM

SUBJECT: Review of Hotline Complaint Concerning Cost and Benefit Estimates for
EPA's Lead-Based Paint Rule
Report No. 12-P-0600

FROM: Arthur A. Elkins, Jr.

TO: Jim Jones
Acting Assistant Administrator for Chemical Safety and Pollution Prevention

This is our report on the subject review conducted by the Office of Inspector General (OIG) of the
U.S. Environmental Protection Agency (EPA). This report contains findings that describe the
problems the OIG has identified and corrective actions the OIG recommends. This report represents
the opinion of the OIG and does not necessarily represent the final EPA position. Final
determinations on matters in this report will be made by EPA managers in accordance with
established resolution procedures.

Action Required

In accordance with EPA Manual 2750, you are required to provide a written response to this report
within 90 calendar days. The recommendations are listed as unresolved with resolution efforts in
progress. Your response should include a corrective action plan for agreed-upon actions, including
actual or estimated milestone completion dates. Your response will be posted on the OIG's public
website, along with our comments to your response. Your response should be provided in an Adobe
PDF file that complies with the accessibility requirements of Section 508 of the Rehabilitation Act of
1973, as amended. Please e-mail your response to Carolyn Copper at copper.carolyn@epa.gov. If your
response contains data that you do not want to be released to the public, you should identify the data
for redaction. We have no objections to the further release of this report to the public.

If you or your staff have any questions regarding this report, please contact Carolyn Copper at
(202) 566-0829 or copper.carolyn@epa.gov, or Patrick Milligan at (215) 814-2326 or
milligan.patrick@epa.gov.

Table of Contents

Chapters

Appendices

Chapter 1
Introduction

Purpose

The U.S. Environmental Protection Agency (EPA), Office of Inspector General (OIG), received a hotline complaint concerning EPA's Lead: Renovation, Repair, and Painting Rule (Lead Rule). The complainant questioned aspects of the rule. Our objective was to evaluate how EPA determined the costs and benefits associated with the Lead Rule. This encompasses the economic analyses for both the 2008 final rule and its 2010 amendment.

Background

The 1992 Residential Lead-Based Paint Hazard Reduction Act established Title IV of the Toxic Substances Control Act (TSCA). TSCA required EPA to issue a rule by 1996 to regulate the lead hazards created from renovation work. In 2005, EPA was sued by environmental groups for failure to issue the Lead Rule by 1996. In a January 2008 settlement agreement, EPA committed to issuing the Lead Rule on or before March 31, 2008. In addition, under the Consolidated Appropriations Act of 2008, the EPA Administrator was directed to finalize the Lead Rule by March 31, 2008. EPA issued the final rule on April 22, 2008.

The purpose of the 2008 Lead Rule was to address lead-based paint hazards created by renovation, repair, and painting activities that disturb lead-based paint in target housing[1] and child-occupied facilities.[2] Under the Lead Rule, firms that perform renovation, repair, or painting activities for compensation in buildings covered by the regulation must be EPA certified, train at least one of their employees as a certified renovator, use a certified renovator to train other workers to perform renovation activities, and ensure that lead-safe work practices are used for projects that disturb lead-based paint.

The 2008 Lead Rule also included an "opt-out" provision. The provision established that Lead Rule training and work practice requirements were

---

[1] Target housing is defined in Section 401 of TSCA as any housing constructed before 1978, except housing for the elderly or persons with disabilities (unless any child under age 6 resides or is expected to reside in such housing) or any 0-bedroom dwelling.

[2] A child-occupied facility is defined under the rule as a building, or portion of a building, constructed prior to 1978, visited regularly by the same child, under 6 years of age, on at least two different days within any week (Sunday through Saturday period), provided that each day's visit lasts at least 3 hours and the combined weekly visits last at least 6 hours, and the combined annual visits last at least 60 hours. Child-occupied facilities may include, but are not limited to, day care centers, preschools, and kindergarten classrooms. Child-occupied facilities may be located in target housing or in public or commercial buildings. (Source: 40 C.F.R. Sec. 745.83)

exempted when a homeowner certifies that no children under age 6 or pregnant women occupy the residence, and the home is not a child-occupied facility. The opt-out provision did not apply to rental housing.

In 2009, in response to lawsuits filed against the 2008 Lead Rule, EPA signed a settlement agreement with public interest groups to amend the rule. The 2010 amendment removed the opt-out provision and imposed additional recordkeeping requirements on renovation firms.

EPA's Economic Analysis for the Lead Rule

Office of Management and Budget (OMB) Circular A-4 provides guidance to federal agencies on the development of rulemaking and regulatory analysis as required under Executive Order 12866. EPA's 2000 *Guidelines for Preparing Economic Analyses* explains that it uses the following three approaches to calculate the economic impacts of a rule before undertaking the rulemaking:

- Benefit-cost analysis—calculates the social benefits and costs of a rule
- Economic impact analysis—examines the gainers and losers of a rule
- Equity assessment—addresses broad concerns such as changes in the national distribution of income or wealth, and can address how policies affect specific sub-populations, including disadvantaged or vulnerable sub-populations.

For the Lead Rule, the benefit-cost analysis contained detailed analysis of the costs to regulated entities of the specific work practices required by the federal rule.

EPA estimated the number of renovation events covered per year, the costs to regulated entities in the first year and on an annualized basis for the first 50 years, and societal benefits for the 2008 Lead Rule. For the 2010 amendment, EPA estimated the number of events and the cost information for the events that would occur from removal of the opt-out provision. See appendix A for more information on EPA's methodology for determining the costs and benefits. Table 1 summarizes the results of EPA's benefit-cost analysis:

Table 1: EPA's cost and benefit estimates for the 2008 Lead Rule and additional costs and benefits of the 2010 amendment

	No. of renovation events covered	Cost to regulated entities, year 1	Cost to regulated entities per year, annualized	Benefits to society
2008 Lead Rule	11.4 million	$758 million	$404 million	$681 million–$1.7 billion
2010 amendment	7.3 million	$507 million	$295 million	$866 million–$3.1 billion
Total	18.7 million	$1.265 billion	$699 million	$1.5 billion–$4.8 billion

Source: EPA Economic Analyses for the 2008 Lead Rule and the 2010 amendment.

Opportunities to Review the Lead Rule

In 2011, Executive Order 13563, *Improving Regulation and Regulatory Review,* directed all federal agencies to develop plans for periodically reviewing existing regulations to determine whether any should be modified, streamlined, expanded, or repealed. In August 2011, EPA issued its final plan for conducting reviews of rulemaking, *Improving Our Regulations: A Preliminary Plan for Periodic Retrospective Reviews of Existing Regulations.* According to its plan, EPA would review 35 rulemakings. Sixteen of the 35 rulemakings were considered "early action" for which EPA intended to propose or finalize an action to modify, streamline, expand, or repeal a regulation or related program. For 5 of those 35 rulemakings,[3] EPA compared cost estimates used in developing the rule with actual costs after the rule had been implemented, to identify possible sources of uncertainty in cost estimates and to look for systematic biases in cost estimates. The 2008 Lead Rule and the 2010 amendment were not included in the scope of EPA's regulatory review activities under Executive Order 13563.

In March 2012, EPA released the interim report, *Retrospective Study of the Costs of EPA Regulations: An Interim Report of Five Case Studies,* for review by the Science Advisory Board Environmental Economics Advisory Committee. The report examines the process and factors that affect the estimated costs of issuing the five regulations. EPA's position is that there are too few analyses after a regulation is in place to draw conclusions regarding general tendencies to under- or over-estimate costs. The insufficiency of data before and after implementation of rules may have contributed to differences in cost and benefit analyses.

A second authority by which EPA can review rules is under Section 610 of the Regulatory Flexibility Act of 1980, as amended by the Small Business Regulatory Enforcement Fairness Act of 1996. The Regulatory Flexibility Act states that each agency shall publish:

> a plan for the periodic review of the rules issued by the agency which have or will have a significant economic impact upon a substantial number of small entities.... The purpose of the review shall be to determine whether such rules should be continued without change, or should be amended or rescinded, consistent with the stated objectives of applicable statutes....

---

[3] The five rules included in this study are: (1) National Primary Drinking Water Regulations; Arsenic and Clarifications to Compliance and New Source Contaminants Monitoring; (2) National Emission Standards for Hazardous Air Pollutants for Source Category: Pulp and Paper Production; Effluent Limitations Guidelines, Pretreatment Standards, and New Source Performance Standards: Pulp, Paper, and Paperboard Category; (3) Revision of Standards of Performance for Nitrogen Oxide Emissions From New Fossil-Fuel Fired Steam Generating Units; Revisions to Reporting Requirements for Standards of Performance for New Fossil-Fuel Fired Steam Generating Units; (4) Emission Standards for Locomotives and Locomotive Engines; and (5) Methyl Bromide Critical Use Nomination for Preplant Soil Use for Strawberry Fruit Grown in Open Fields (Submitted in 2003 for the 2006 Use Season).

The Regulatory Flexibility Act, as amended, directs the consideration of, among other things, the nature of complaints or comments received concerning the rule from the public; and the length of time since the rule has been evaluated or the degree to which technology, economic conditions, or other factors have changed in the area affected by the rule.

Scope and Methodology

We conducted our evaluation from December 21, 2010, to February 13, 2012. We performed our work in accordance with generally accepted government auditing standards issued by the Comptroller General of the United States. Those standards require that we plan and perform the review to obtain sufficient, appropriate evidence to provide a reasonable basis for our findings and conclusions based on our review objectives. We believe that the evidence obtained provides a reasonable basis for our findings and conclusions based on our review objectives.

The scope of our review included EPA's April 22, 2008, Lead; Renovation, Repair, and Painting Program Rule; and the Rule's May 6, 2010, amendment. To accomplish our objective and address the hotline complaint, we reviewed EPA rulemaking documents obtained from the http://www.regulations.gov website and from EPA. These documents included the April 22, 2008, Lead Rule and the May 6, 2010, amendment; the economic analyses for both the Lead Rule[4] and its amendment,[5] and the Agency's 2008 and 2010 responses to public comments. The OIG did not examine whether EPA complied with all aspects of federal rulemaking guidance and procedures. We reviewed those aspects of rulemaking necessary to address the hotline complaint.

We interviewed EPA staff in the Office of Chemical Safety and Pollution Prevention at headquarters, including the Director of Economics Exposure and Technology Division, the Director of Regulatory Coordination, and the economist responsible for developing the economic analyses. We also obtained information from the EPA contractor who performed the work practices survey for EPA's 2008 Lead Rule.

We reviewed EPA's 2000 guidance for the preparation of economic analyses, OMB's Circular A-4 rulemaking guidance, and the statutory requirements regarding the preparation of economic analyses. We reviewed EPA's explanation in the economic analyses for how it calculated the cost and the benefits for both the Lead Rule and the amendment. We focused on EPA's benefit-cost analysis for the 2008 rule and its 2010 amendment because it provided the estimated costs of specific rule requirements and estimates of certain rule benefits. We also reviewed other chapters of the 2008 economic analysis that discussed the economic impact analysis and the equity assessment.

---

[4] *The Lead Rule: The Economic Analysis for the TSCA Lead Renovation, Repair, and Painting Program Final Rule for Target Housing and Child-Occupied Facilities*, March 2008.

[5] *The Amendment: The Economic Analysis for the TSCA Lead Renovation, Repair, and Painting Program Opt-out and Recordkeeping Proposed Rule for Target Housing and Child Occupied Facilities*, October 2009.

Chapter 2
Some of the Data on Which EPA Based Its Cost and Benefit Estimates for the Lead Rule Were Limited

EPA used limited data to develop its cost and benefit estimates for the 2008 Lead Rule. The Agency used self-reported information from only nine businesses to estimate the incremental work practice costs and benefits of the Lead Rule. EPA's contractor said it contacted a couple of hundred businesses to find nine who would provide information. We believe this to be limited information. On the basis of this limited information, EPA concluded that many lead-safe work practices were already being used by renovation businesses and, therefore, the costs of the Lead Rule were "relatively low." Further, this conclusion appears to have led EPA to exclude other potential costs from its analysis. In addition, the Agency's Clean Air Scientific Advisory Committee (CASAC)[6] reported that EPA's data for estimating intelligence quotient (IQ) changes in children exposed to lead dust during renovations would not adequately support a rigorous cost-benefit analysis. We did not conclude that EPA violated policies or failed to follow requirements in conducting its analysis, but was under pressure to issue the rule and used its discretion in performing the economic analysis using some limited data.

Limitations in Cost Analysis

In its economic analysis of the Lead Rule, EPA acknowledged that the survey data that contributed to the basis of its cost estimate did not come from a statistically valid survey, and there is considerable uncertainty associated with the work practices identified through the survey. EPA's initial determination that the costs of the Lead Rule were relatively low appears to have contributed to successive assumptions that other potential rule costs did not need to be considered.

EPA's Incremental Cost Estimates for Lead-Safe Work Practices Derived From a Survey of Nine Businesses

According to EPA, 323,147 businesses would be impacted by the Lead Rule. In 2007, an EPA contractor conducted a limited, non-random, survey of painting and residential general contractors to identify those lead-safe renovation practices that were already being used by renovation contractors. EPA would use that information to estimate the incremental costs to comply with the new rule requirements. An EPA manager said that under the Paperwork Reduction Act, EPA could only survey nine businesses unless it submitted an application for an

---

[6] CASAC is a federal advisory committee that is chartered to provide scientific information and advice to the EPA Administrator.

exemption, also known as an Information Collection Request, to OMB. Another EPA manager added that based on past experience, obtaining OMB approval for an Information Collection Request and then conducting the survey could take up to 2 years to complete, which would have greatly exceeded the time frame for issuing the rule EPA agreed to in its settlement agreement. Consequently, EPA elected to perform a limited survey of nine firms.

To determine the nine firms to survey, the EPA contractor that conducted the survey stated that a "couple of hundred" businesses were contacted, and the first nine businesses that agreed to participate in the survey became the survey participants. EPA's non-probability sample selection of the first nine firms that would respond is not a sampling method that supports a determination that the sample was representative of the more than 300,000 firms EPA acknowledged would be impacted by the rule. EPA's selection of the first nine firms that responded represents a convenience sample. Convenience samples should not be used to develop generalizations about the target population. Random samples, when drawn properly, can be used to accurately estimate characteristics of the target population such as, in this case, what lead-safe work practices were already in use. These are basic and documented principles of survey research, as indicated by OMB and others.[7]

To arrive at its incremental cost estimates for lead-safe work practices, EPA first estimated the cost of each required work practice for several types and sizes of renovation jobs. EPA then assessed the extent to which lead-safe work practices were already being used by the nine survey respondents. The survey information showed that, on average, more than 75 percent of the nine firms already used lead-safe work practices, such as covering floors with taped-down plastic sheeting and vacuuming surfaces in the work area. In its economic analysis of the Lead Rule, EPA acknowledged that the survey data were not based on a statistically valid survey and that there is considerable uncertainty associated with the work practices identified through the survey. Nevertheless, EPA used the survey results to establish the baseline for estimating the cost to comply with the work practices required by the Lead Rule. Based on those results, EPA concluded that there would be relatively low incremental costs associated with the rule because contractors would need to make few changes from their current work practices to comply.

Some Opportunity Costs Excluded From EPA's Analysis

EPA's initial decision that the costs of the Lead Rule were relatively low appears to have contributed to successive assumptions that other potential rule costs did not need to be considered. For example, the Agency decided that it did not need to quantify some opportunity costs associated with implementation of the Lead Rule.

---

[7] See *OMB Guidance on Agency Survey and Statistical Information Collections*, http://www.whitehouse.gov/sites/default/files/omb/inforeg/pmc_survey_guidance_2006.pdf; and *Introduction to Sampling for Non-Statisticians*, Safaa R. Amer, Senior Statistician, National Opinion Research Center, University of Chicago, February 2011, http://www.amstat.org/sections/srms/IntroductiontoSamplingforNon-Statisticians.pdf.

Opportunity costs are the value of the goods and services lost by society resulting from resources being used to comply with and implement the rule. EPA's *2000 Guidelines for Preparing Economic Analyses* states, in part, that the goal of a benefit-cost analysis is to determine the net change in social welfare brought about by a new environmental policy. When determining the cost impacts of the Lead Rule, EPA did not include estimates for three categories of opportunity costs:

- Social welfare costs, which are increased consumer and producer prices and legal and administrative costs
- Transitional costs, such as unemployment, firms closing, and resource shifts to other markets
- Other indirect costs, which are changes in markets indirectly affected by the rule

In its response to public comments on both the rule and the amendment, EPA noted that the Lead Rule would not affect consumer options or the cost of renovations because it believed that contractors' costs to comply with the Lead Rule would be relatively low. EPA concluded that the number of renovations would not change and, consequently, there would not be a loss of renovation jobs or an impact on transitional costs. EPA also told the OIG that it concluded there would be relatively few adverse affects on markets that are indirectly affected by the rule. However, we believe that the rule may affect consumer decisions on whether to have renovation work performed by a compliant contractor or whether to undertake the work at all. Therefore, some opportunity costs affecting consumer and supplier resources and potential unemployment should have been considered in estimating the costs.

Additional Contractor Liability Insurance Costs Excluded From EPA's Analysis

In the economic analysis, EPA did not include the cost of contractors' additional liability insurance in the cost of complying with the Lead Rule. EPA did not include insurance as a cost because the Lead Rule does not require contractors to purchase insurance. Also, according to EPA and OMB guidance, the cost of insurance is considered a "transfer" among parties. EPA rule-making staff said these transfers do not affect costs because premiums are paid to insurance companies that return the premiums to society when claims are submitted. They also said that this is how insurance costs are handled in EPA rulemakings, and that other federal agencies do the same.

According to OMB guidance for Executive Order 12866, transfers should not be included in the estimates of benefits and costs of a regulation. Instead, they should be addressed as part of the regulation's distributional effects (how both benefits and costs are distributed among subpopulations of particular concern). However, EPA did not address additional insurance costs in the Lead Rule's distributional analysis (which comprises the economic impact analysis and the equity assessment).

EPA believes that contractors' use of lead-safe work practices would lessen their potential liability. Yet, according to public comments for the Lead Rule and its amendment, renovators listed additional liability insurance as a cost that firms would incur.

Costs Associated with EPA-Recommended Work Practices Excluded From EPA's Analysis

We found that EPA presented or recommended additional work practices in a mandatory training program on how to comply with the Lead Rule. However, these work practices are not required by the rule and are not included in the rule's costs to comply.

EPA, in collaboration with the U.S. Department of Housing and Urban Development, developed the "Lead Safety for Renovation Repair and Painting" training course to train renovation, repair, and painting contractors on how to work safely in housing with lead-based paint. The instructor manual for the training course was issued in February 2009. The manual lists some Occupational Safety and Health Administration requirements for meeting the "Lead in Construction Standard," and some U.S. Department of Housing and Urban Development requirements for meeting the "Lead-Safe Housing Rule." Apart from these Occupational Safety and Health Administration and U.S. Department of Housing and Urban Development requirements, the training manual includes three categories of work practices:

- Work practices "required" to comply with the Lead Rule
- "Recommended" work practices
- Work practices presented during the certification training that were not labeled "required" or "recommended" (these are "other" work practices)

EPA only included the activities and equipment that are designated "required" in its cost estimate for the Lead Rule.

In our opinion, contractors may see little if any distinction between something EPA "requires" versus something it "recommends." EPA has authority to penalize renovation firms that do not perform lead-safe renovations as required in the rule. Consequently, we believe that all the work practices presented in the EPA training are practices that contractors may implement and that may result in additional costs to business, although these practices were not accounted for in the rule. In addition, contractors may believe that they could be liable for not adequately protecting the homeowner or workers from exposure to lead if they do not perform a work practice that has been documented as "EPA recommended."

EPA is aware that some contractors have adopted some EPA-recommended and other work practices, and EPA acknowledges that the additional costs associated with those practices are not included in its analysis. Examples of the recommended and other work practices that EPA identifies in the training but does not include in cost estimates are:

- Attaching plastic sheeting to the exterior of the window
- Using precautions such as baby wipes to ensure that all personnel, tools, and other items are free of dust and debris
- Removing toys and other items from the work area
- Covering all play areas, including sandboxes
- Using a shroud for HEPA[8]-filtered tools
- Using a second smaller layer of protective sheeting with chemical strippers
- Cleaning tools at the end of the day
- Washing hands each time workers leave the work area

Limitations in Benefit Analysis

In its economic analysis for the 2008 Lead Rule, EPA stated that the rule would generate substantial benefits. However, EPA also acknowledged that it has limited confidence in the stated benefits because it had not determined why the benefits analyses contained unusual results.

EPA's Clean Air Act Scientific Committee (CASAC) identified several issues with EPA's plan to analyze the estimated benefits from the rule. CASAC noted that although the overall concepts in EPA's approach were reasonable, CASAC could not endorse the specific steps, procedures, and data analyses contained in the Agency's draft methodology document, which was used to develop estimates for the benefits section of the Economic Analysis.

The benefits analysis is based on three main components: the dust study, blood lead-IQ modeling, and benefits estimation. The November 2007 *Revised Final Report on Characterization of Dust Lead Levels after Renovation, Repair, and Painting Activities* (hereafter referred to as the dust study) was designed to characterize dust lead levels during various renovation, repair, and painting activities.

CASAC found that the dust study was reasonably well designed considering the complexity of the problem, and that the report provided information not available from any other source. CASAC noted that of particular interest was the impact of specific work practices that would be required under the proposed rule. CASAC also cited the dust study as providing input for the type of exposure data needed for the draft Lead Rule. However, CASAC stated that the limited data included in the dust study most likely rendered the study not statistically valid or nationally representative.

---

[8] HEPA stands for high-efficiency particulate air.

Most of the structures used in the dust study were built prior to the 1930s, and the primary estimate did not reflect changes over time in lead levels in paint. EPA accounted for the variation in lead levels in paint over time in its sensitivity analysis, which resulted in a 14 percent reduction in benefits. However, EPA did not include this reduction when it calculated the estimated benefits for the Lead Rule.

EPA's estimation of benefits[9] is based on the value of reduced lifetime earnings due to IQ loss from exposures to children under the age of 6. EPA used its blood lead–IQ modeling approach as part of the analysis to calculate the expected benefits from the Lead Rule. EPA ran multiple exposure scenarios, changing key variables such as the type of renovation job or combination of jobs, the age of the child, workspace assumptions, and other factors. Under each of these scenarios, EPA calculated the change in IQ points and weighed the results according to the number of children exposed to a given scenario. Finally, EPA assigned a dollar value to monetize the aggregate loss in IQ points.

CASAC found that the data were inadequate to support the proposed modeling approach for estimating the IQ changes in children exposed during renovations. Further, EPA's benefits analysis identified that some results were unexpected; for example, the modeling results showed that only using containment at a work site would yield higher benefits than if the contractor also cleaned and verified that no lead was present. In its analysis, EPA noted that these types of unreasonable results are likely due to underlying data and modeling assumptions. EPA also acknowledged that it did not investigate all possible data or modeling assumptions to determine the cause of the inconsistent results. EPA acknowledged that more representative data would have been desirable, but that the Agency had to proceed with the best information available at that time.

Conclusions

EPA concluded that work practice costs for businesses to comply with the Lead Rule were relatively low. This decision influenced other discretionary EPA actions to exclude potential additional costs of the rule. In addition, EPA's decision to include non-mandatory work practices in official training programs may result in additional unaccounted-for costs that would be incurred by businesses that attempt to comply with EPA training guidance. Sound data on the rule's benefits were also not available at the time of the rulemaking, and this limitation was known to EPA and its scientific advisory committee. However, EPA went forward with the rule because its benefit-cost analysis indicated that the rule generated substantial benefits, and because EPA was legally obligated to issue the rule.

---

[9] In the Executive Summary of the 2008 rule, EPA cited other health benefits such as cardiovascular benefits.

We have identified only a few aspects of EPA's complex benefit-cost analysis that are limited. However, we believe these aspects limit the reliability of EPA's estimates of the rule's costs and benefits to society. The Administration's 2011 Executive Order and Section 610 of the Regulatory Flexibility Act provide EPA an opportunity to review the Lead Rule to determine whether it should be modified, streamlined, expanded, or repealed in light of the known limitations in the rule's underlying cost and benefit estimates. OMB seeks to create a culture of retrospective analysis in which existing rules (whether issued in the recent past or decades ago) are subject to assessment and continuing evaluation, with public input.

Recommendations

We recommend that the Assistant Administrator for Chemical Safety and Pollution Prevention:

1. Consistent with a retrospective and flexible EPA regulatory culture, reexamine the estimated costs and benefits of the 2008 Lead Rule and the 2010 amendment to determine whether the rule should be modified, streamlined, expanded, or repealed.

2. Add a disclaimer to the February 2009 instructor manual, *Lead Safety for Renovation, Repair, and Painting,* to communicate the difference between required and recommended work practices. The disclaimer should state that EPA did not consider the costs and benefits of any non-required work practices in developing the rule and that required work practices in the training manual must be performed to comply with the law.

Agency Response and OIG Evaluation

We received comments from the Acting Assistant Administrator for Chemical Safety and Pollution Prevention. For recommendation 1, the Agency responded that the OIG's draft report contains a number of inaccurate statements that contributed to inappropriate conclusions and recommendations. As a result, the Agency strongly disagrees with the first recommendation of the report, that the office re-examine the costs and benefits of the 2008 rule and 2010 amendments.

The Inspector General met with the Acting Assistant Administrator for Chemical Safety and Pollution Prevention on May 25, 2012, to discuss the Office of Chemical Safety and Pollution Prevention's response to the draft report. The Acting Assistant Administrator said his office did not agree with recommendation 1 because the office did not believe it was cost effective to take a retrospective look at the economic analysis for the Lead Rule because, even if the cost estimates were understated, the benefits estimate would still significantly outweigh the costs. In the written response to the draft report, the Agency stated that its economic analysis was appropriate to support decisions made by Agency officials responsible for the lead-based paint rulemaking, was conducted according to Agency guidelines, was subject to public comment, and was cleared by OMB as complying with the requirements of Executive Order 12866.

We agree that the economic analysis was conducted according to Agency guidelines, was subject to public comment, and was cleared by OMB as complying with the requirements of Executive Order 12866. However, this does not mean that the economic analysis was without limitations. It appears that in reviewing and responding to our report, EPA has confused OIG's findings about limitations in the Agency's economic and benefits analysis as meaning that the Agency's analysis and rulemaking actions violated policies or guidance. The OIG did not find or state this. The purpose of this OIG hotline review was to evaluate how EPA determined the costs and benefits associated with the Lead Rule. Our evaluation identified limitations in EPA's analysis.

EPA's approach in conducting its analysis for this rule was constrained by time pressure and mandated deadlines for performance, which resulted in reliance on limited data to draw conclusions about the rule's costs and benefits. OMB reports indicate that reliance on limited data is not necessarily uncommon in the federal rulemaking analysis. We maintain our position on recommendation 1 that EPA reexamine the costs and benefits of the rule given the known and disclosed uncertainties and limitations. Our recommendation aligns with recently established federal government requirements to conduct retrospective analysis of federal agency rules. In addition, our recommendation aligns with requirements of Section 610 of the Regulatory Flexibility Act of 1980, as amended by the Small Business Regulatory Enforcement Fairness Act of 1996. In the final report, recommendation 1 is designated as unresolved with resolution efforts in progress.

For recommendation 2, the Office of Chemical Safety and Pollution Prevention agreed that it is important for renovators to clearly understand what practices are required by the Renovation, Repair, and Painting Rule. The office stated that, in part due to feedback from renovators and training providers, EPA revised the *Lead Safety for Renovation, Repair and Painting* instructor manual in October 2011 to clarify the distinction of required versus recommended work practices.

EPA's revisions to the training manual occurred after we notified the Agency of this issue and provided it with a draft recommendation on September 1, 2011. In its 90-day response to the final report, EPA should describe the specific manual revisions they implemented. This will allow the OIG to determine whether the revisions to the training manual meet the intent of the recommendation. In the final report, recommendation 2 is designated as unresolved with resolution efforts in progress.

Status of Recommendations and Potential Monetary Benefits

		RECOMMENDATIONS				POTENTIAL MONETARY BENEFITS (in $000s)	
Rec. No.	Page No.	Subject	Status[1]	Action Official	Planned Completion Date	Claimed Amount	Agreed To Amount
1	11	Consistent with a retrospective and flexible EPA regulatory culture, reexamine the estimated costs and benefits of the 2008 Lead Rule and the 2010 amendment to determine whether the rule should be modified, streamlined, expanded, or repealed.	U	Assistant Administrator for Chemical Safety and Pollution Prevention			
2	11	Add a disclaimer to the February 2009 instructor manual, *Lead Safety for Renovation, Repair, and Painting*, to communicate the difference between required and recommended work practices. The disclaimer should state that EPA did not consider the costs and benefits of any non-required work practices in developing the rule and that required work practices in the training manual must be performed to comply with the law.	U	Assistant Administrator for Chemical Safety and Pollution Prevention			

[1] O = recommendation is open with agreed-to corrective actions pending
   C = recommendation is closed with all agreed-to actions completed
   U = recommendation is unresolved with resolution efforts in progress

EPA's Methodology for Calculating Costs and Benefits of the Lead Rule

Cost Methodology

EPA divided the costs associated with the regulatory impact of the 2008 Lead Rule into four categories for the purposes of the economic analysis: (1) work practice costs, (2) training costs, (3) certification costs (which include the firm's paperwork burden and EPA administrative and enforcement costs), and (4) pre-renovation education costs. EPA's general approach was to first estimate the number of affected activities or entities, and then estimate the incremental regulatory cost per activity or entity affected. Finally, the incremental costs and the number of affected activities and entities were combined to estimate the total costs. EPA calculated the costs, benefits, and small-entity[10] impacts assuming a 75 percent compliance rate with the rule's requirements. The analysis first estimates the total costs associated with the first 4 years of regulation, and then extrapolates to the costs of the regulation over a 50-year period, estimated with 3 percent and 7 percent discount rates.

In calculating the cost for the 2010 amendment, the change in the costs associated with work practices, training, and certification were all attributable to the elimination of the opt-out provision, which extends the 2008 Lead Rule requirements to additional housing units. In addition to the work practice costs associated with the renovation, repair, and painting events in these housing units, this change is expected to result in more individuals and firms seeking training and certification. The fourth category of analysis for the amendment—recordkeeping checklist provision costs—applies to all housing units regulated under the 2008 Lead Rule as well as the additional housing units that would no longer be eligible for the opt-out provision. EPA's general approach for estimating the costs for the 2010 amendment are the same as for the 2008 rule.

Benefit Methodology

The benefits for the 2008 Lead Rule are a result of the reduction in adverse health effects due to decreased exposure to lead dust. There are five primary steps in estimating the adverse health effects associated with renovation, repair, and painting projects:

- Mapping renovation, repair, and painting activities into dust study activities and then generating the universe of renovation, repair, and paint exposure scenarios for which IQ change will be estimated.
- Estimating the child-specific IQ change per each renovation, repair, and paint exposure scenario generated in step 1, while taking into account age of the child, workspace access, and vintage of the building.
- Defining the current work practice baseline (cleaning and containment).

---

[10] Small entities are small businesses, small governmental jurisdictions, and/or small not-for-profit organizations.

- Scaling up the incremental IQ change values for each regulatory option to capture the population of children affected by all renovation, repair, and paint events disturbing lead-based paint.
- Multiplying the population-based IQ change by the value of an IQ point. The estimated value of an IQ point is $12,953 (2005 dollars).[11]

The 2010 economic analysis[12] benefits calculation for children under the age of 6 were based on avoided losses in expected earnings due to drop, and the calculations for adults were based on the avoided medical costs (or other proxies for willingness to pay) for hypertension, coronary heart disease, stroke, and the resulting incidence of deaths.

EPA calculated benefits numbers for several groups of individuals protected by removing the opt-out provision. The first step in calculating the benefits for the 2010 analysis was to estimate the number of individuals who would be protected by eliminating the opt-out provision. EPA did this by estimating the number of affected housing units. Next, EPA estimated the number of occupants in the affected households. Then, EPA estimated the number of individuals protected as the number of individuals who reside where lead-based paint is disturbed during renovation, repair, and painting. Finally, EPA multiplied the number of individuals by the average benefit per individual.

---

[11] This estimated value is derived from coefficients provided by Salkever, D.S., 1995. Updated estimates of earnings benefits from reduced exposure of children to environmental lead. Environmental Research 70 (1): 1–6.
[12] The economic analysis for the 2010 amendment titled, "Economic Analysis for the TSCA Lead Renovation, Repair, and Painting Program Opt-out and Recordkeeping Proposed Rule for Target Housing and Child-Occupied Facilities," was completed in October 2009.

Agency Response to Draft Report and OIG Evaluation

March 27 2012

MEMORANDUM

SUBJECT: Response to OIG Hotline Complaint Concerning EPA's Lead Based Paint Rule, Assignment OPE-FY11-006

FROM: James J. Jones, Acting Assistant Administrator
Office of Chemical Safety and Pollution Prevention

TO: Arthur A. Elkins, Jr.
Inspector General

This memorandum is in response to the Office of Inspector General's (OIG) February 13, 2012, Draft Report entitled "Review of Hotline Complaint Concerning EPA's Lead-Based Paint Rule (Project No. 2011-027)". I appreciate the opportunity for the Office of Chemical Safety and Pollution Prevention (OCSPP) to comment on this Draft Report.

Unfortunately, the Draft Report contains a number of inaccurate statements which contribute to inappropriate conclusions and recommendations. As a result, I strongly disagree with the first recommendation of the report, that the Office re-examine the costs and benefits of the 2008 rule and 2010 amendments.

The economic analysis was appropriate to support decisions made by Agency officials responsible for the Lead-Based Paint Rulemaking, was conducted according to Agency guidelines, was subject to public comment, and was cleared by the Office of Management and Budget as complying with the requirements of EO 12866.

OIG Response 1: The OIG has carefully reviewed the Agency's response. We agree that the economic analysis was generally conducted according to Agency guidelines; was subject to public comment; and, according to EPA, was cleared by OMB as complying with the requirements of Executive Order 12866. However, this does not mean that the economic analysis was without limitations. It appears that in reviewing and responding to our report, EPA has confused OIG's findings about limitations in the Agency's economic and benefits analysis as meaning that the Agency's analysis and rulemaking actions violated policies or guidance. However, OIG did not find or state this. The purpose of this OIG hotline review was to evaluate how EPA determined the costs and benefits associated with the Lead Rule. Our evaluation identified limitations in EPA's analysis. We recognize that EPA's approach in conducting its analysis for this rule was constrained by time pressure and mandated deadlines for performance. We maintain that on the basis of a limited survey, EPA concluded that work practice costs for business to comply with the Lead Rule were relatively low. This decision influenced other discretionary EPA actions to exclude potential additional costs of the rule. EPA acknowledged that the survey data contributed to the basis of its cost estimate and that the data did not come from a statistically valid survey, and that there is considerable uncertainty associated with the work practices identified through the survey. Therefore, we conclude that EPA's initial determination that the costs of the Lead Rule were relatively low appears to have contributed to successive assumptions that other potential rule costs did not need to be considered.

According to OMB's "Draft 2012 Report to Congress on the Benefits and Costs of Federal Regulations and Unfunded Mandates on State, Local, and Tribal Entities," quantification of the costs and benefits of some rules is highly speculative, often because information does not exist. There are, at times, real and immovable obstacles to federal agencies' abilities to obtain the data necessary to make non-speculative decisions about the costs and benefits of federal rules. OMB's report states that, "It is not unusual for agencies to issue rules with at least a degree of uncertainty about one or another provision." Consequently, as described by OMB, Executive Order 13563 (Improving Regulation and Regulatory Review), established requirements for federal agencies to conduct 'retrospective' analysis of significant federal rules "to determine whether any such regulations should be modified, streamlined, expanded, or repealed so as to make the agency's regulatory program more effective or less burdensome in achieving the regulatory objectives." OMB seeks to create a culture of retrospective analysis in which existing rules (whether issued in the very recent past or decades ago) are subject to assessment and continuing evaluation, with public input. OMB recommends that retrospective analysis should become a routine part of agency rulemaking and that formal mechanisms should be maintained to regularly reevaluate rules that may be unjustified, excessive, insufficient, or unduly complex.

We maintain our position on our first recommendation that EPA reexamine the costs and benefits of the rule, given the known and disclosed uncertainties and limitations. Our recommendation aligns with recently established federal government requirements to conduct retrospective analysis of federal agency rules. In addition, our recommendation aligns with requirements of Section 610 of the Regulatory Flexibility Act of 1980, as amended by the Small Business

-continued-

Regulatory Enforcement Fairness Act of 1996. The Regulatory Flexibility Act states that each agency shall publish:

> a plan for the periodic review of the rules issued by the agency which have or will have a significant economic impact upon a substantial number of small entities.... The purpose of the review shall be to determine whether such rules should be continued without change, or should be amended or rescinded, consistent with the stated objectives of applicable statutes....

The Regulatory Flexibility Act, as amended, directs the consideration of, among other things, the nature of complaints or comments received concerning the rule from the public, and the length of time since the rule has been evaluated or the degree to which technology, economic conditions, or other factors have changed in the area affected by the rule.

Additional clarifications are discussed in more detail in the attached document.

The Draft Report's second recommendation is that OCSPP should add a disclaimer to the instructor manual communicating the difference between required and recommended work practices. The instructor manual is designed to present Training Providers with tools to communicate the necessity of performing required work practices in order to comply with the regulations. Information related to the economic analysis is not appropriate for such communication. However, we agree that it is important for renovators to clearly understand what practices are required by the Renovation, Repair, and Painting Rule. In part due to feedback from renovators and training providers, EPA revised the *Lead Safety for Renovation, Repair and Painting* instructor manual in October 2011 to clarify the distinction of required versus recommended work practices.

OIG Response 2: EPA's revisions to the training manual occurred after we notified the Agency of this issue and provided EPA with a draft recommendation on September 1, 2011. In its 90-day response to the final report, EPA should describe the specific manual revisions it implemented. This will allow the OIG to determine whether the revisions to the training manual meet the intent of the recommendation. In the final report, this recommendation is designated as unresolved with resolution efforts in progress.

Thank you again for the opportunity to comment on this Draft Report. I look forward to working with your office as the report is finalized. If you have questions, please feel free to contact me, or to have your staff contact Janet Weiner of my staff at (202) 564-2309.

OCSPP RESPONSE TO DRAFT REPORT
PROJECT NO. 2011-027
March 26, 2012

This document summarizes OCSPP's position regarding the Draft Report entitled "Review of Hotline Complaint Concerning EPA's Lead Based Paint Rule," dated February 13, 2012. In summary, EPA believes the recommendations in the Draft Report to be inappropriate, and disagrees that the evidence provides a reasonable basis for OIG's findings and conclusions. For the convenience of the reader, the structure of our comments tracks the format of the Draft Report.

OIG Response 3: OIG has carefully reviewed EPA's response and maintains its position on the two report recommendations. Despite its statement directly above, EPA agrees with our second recommendation and reports that it has taken actions to implement it. Generally accepted government auditing standards require that we plan and perform our work to provide a reasonable basis for our findings and conclusions, based on our review objectives. This determination has been established by trained and knowledgeable OIG professional audit staff.

Our review objective, based on an OIG hotline complaint, was to evaluate how EPA determined the costs and benefits of the Lead Rule. This encompasses the economic analyses for both the 2008 final rule and its 2010 amendment. Our evaluation identified known and documented limitations. It also identified current federal requirements for retrospective analysis of federal rules which provide a reasonable and appropriate means for EPA to determine whether the known limitations in their economic and benefits analysis indicate the need to modify, streamline, expand, or repeal the Lead Rule to make it more effective or less burdensome. In addition, our evaluation identifies a federal requirement under Section 610 of the Regulatory Flexibility Act of 1980, as amended by the Small Business Regulatory Enforcement Fairness Act of 1996. The Regulatory Flexibility Act requires that each agency publish a plan for the periodic review of the rules issued by the agency which have or will have a significant economic impact upon a substantial number of small entities. The purpose of the review shall be to determine whether such rules should be continued without change, or should be amended or rescinded, consistent with the stated objectives of applicable statutes. Fulfilling the requirements of the Regulatory Flexibility Act is also a reasonable and appropriate means EPA can use to address the OIG's first recommendation.

SECTION BY SECTION ANALYSIS:

Limitations in Cost Analysis

EPA's Incremental Cost Estimates for Lead-Safe Work Practices Derived from a Survey of Nine Businesses

The Draft Report states that the sample size of the 2007 survey limited EPA's ability to adequately estimate the costs and benefits of the Lead Rule under Executive Order 12866.

EPA disagrees. The Agency conducted a sensitivity analysis to analyze the impact of possible over reporting or under-reporting of workplace practices. EPA performed a sensitivity analysis in the 2008 Economic Analysis, estimating benefits if work practices required by the rule were used in the baseline with 50 percent greater or lesser frequency than indicated by the survey of 9 renovators. Because a decrease in the assumed baseline level of work practice use increases benefits and costs by about the same amount, the net benefits estimate changed by only 5 percent and were still approximately $1.2 billion per year. This argues against the proposition that a larger survey would have changed the conclusion that the benefits of the rule significantly outweigh the costs.

OIG Response 4: The OIG draft report does not state that the sample size of the 2007 survey limited EPA's ability to adequately estimate the costs and benefits of the Lead Rule under Executive Order 12866. The OIG draft report stated that EPA's assumption that the costs of the rule were low affected its decisions and limited its approach in estimating the cost of the rule.

The OIG draft report does not speculate the results of a larger survey compared to the results of a limited survey of nine participants. However, in discussions with the OIG, EPA managers acknowledged their preference for a large survey over a small survey. The draft report recognizes that EPA acknowledged the limitations of a survey of nine including considerable uncertainty associated with the work practices identified through the survey. With such a limited survey, EPA did not know whether a representative sample of renovation firms was being surveyed. The sensitivity analysis provides useful information on the uncertainties in the cost and benefit analysis. However, it does not address the assumptions and limitations associated with conducting a non-representative survey.

Footnote 1:
The Draft Report fails to mention that EPA tried unsuccessfully to supplement the survey it conducted for the proposed rule by asking for additional information from the industry. In the preamble to the 2006 proposed rule (71 Federal Register 1621) EPA specifically requested comments and supporting information on the extent to which renovators already used the work practices EPA was proposing to require. However, EPA did not receive data about these activities in response to this request. Because of the failure of this request to generate useful information, EPA decided to perform another survey for the final rule.

OIG Response 5: EPA officials informed us that the Agency was under time constraints to issue the final rule because of a January 2008 settlement agreement to issue the Lead Rule on or before March 31, 2008. The OIG recognizes that agencies can encounter obstacles to obtaining necessary and quality information for rulemakings. However, with new federal requirements to conduct retrospective analysis of existing rules, and existing requirements under the Regulatory Flexibility Act, opportunities exist to assess the possible implications that data limitations have for effective and fair federal rules.

The Draft Report contends that EPA's survey was limited because it did not incorporate questions such as the number of employees or annual revenues of the businesses, or what portion of the business was accounted for by renovations on pre-1978 housing.

EPA disagrees, and is not aware of any evidence that the number of employees or the annual revenues of renovators differentially influence the use of containment and cleaning practices. OIG has provided no factual support for its position that this information is relevant to determining whether the surveyed firms were representative of the industry. Furthermore, the survey specifically asked about work practices in pre-1978 housing and COFs. EPA is not aware of any evidence that the baseline work practices used in pre-1978 houses and COFs (which may contain lead-based paint) systematically differ from the baseline work practices used in houses and COFs built after 1978 (when lead-containing paint was banned).

OIG Response 6: The draft report has been clarified to facilitate understanding of the fundamental limitations of the survey. As EPA itself has acknowledged, its survey was not statistically valid. EPA selected a non-probability, convenience sample of nine renovation firms, from more than 300,000, to determine the lead-safe work practices already being used. However, non-random, convenience samples cannot be assumed to be representative of the characteristics of the population of renovation firms.

Some Opportunity Costs Excluded From EPA's Analysis:

The Draft Report asserts that EPA's survey results were responsible for the conclusion that the costs of the RRP program were relatively low, and thus that other potential costs did not need to be considered.

EPA disagrees with this assertion. In fact, EPA's conclusion that the rule's requirements are relatively inexpensive applies irrespective of the assumptions about baseline practices. The cost of the common work practices for the various types of model jobs in the economic analysis varied from \$35 to \$400 per job if the renovator did not perform any cleaning or containment in the baseline, and EPA considers these costs to be low, based on their contribution to the total cost of a renovation project. To put these costs into context, a study by the Joint Center for Housing Studies of Harvard University on *Foundations for Future Growth in the Remodeling Industry* found that the average cost of professional home improvement job was \$9,620. While there can be considerable differences from one job to another, the typical cost of compliance with the RRP rule is small compared to the rest of the cost of a renovation, even if there was no cleaning or containment in the baseline. These costs are not expected to impact the overall costs of renovations.

OIG Response 7: The draft report did not make any assertions about the RRP (Renovation, Repair, and Paint) program as a whole. The objective of our work was to evaluate how EPA determined the costs and benefits associated with the Lead Rule. The draft report also did not assert that EPA's survey results were responsible for the conclusion that the costs of the RRP program were relatively low. The draft report describes the impact of the survey results in a more specific aspect—estimating the cost to comply with the work practices required by the Lead Rule. There are several other cost components that EPA assessed in the rule's economic analysis, such as training costs, certification, and pre-renovation education costs.

The Draft Report states that EPA did not include estimates for three categories of costs: social welfare costs, transition costs, and other indirect costs.

EPA notes that the Draft Report does not present any data indicating that these costs are of significance for the RRP rule. For example, the Report states that EPA did not include administrative costs, but does not specify what specific administrative costs would be incurred that were not already included in EPA's analysis. If such costs even exist in this instance, the Draft Report has not demonstrated that their magnitude is sufficient to be relevant.

OIG Response 8: Our objective was to evaluate how EPA determined the costs and benefits associated with the Lead Rule based on a hotline complaint. OIG performs oversight of EPA activities and operations and, consistent with our objective, we are not responsible for providing the Agency with industry data. It is EPA's responsibility to demonstrate why there would be no impact on the three categories of costs: social welfare costs, transition costs, and other indirect costs.

EPA's Guidelines for Preparing Economic Analyses identifies an array of costs that might be relevant to analyze, at the discretion of the economist. EPA concluded that it was not necessary to attempt to quantify all of these costs, as EPA either did not believe that such costs would be incurred in this situation or that they were sizable enough to make a significant difference in the conclusions drawn from the analysis.

OIG Response 9: The OIG agrees that according to EPA's *2000 Guidelines for Preparing Economic Analyses*, the Agency has discretion for identifying those costs that are relevant to analyze when issuing a rule. We also agree that EPA used its discretion to conclude that it was not necessary to attempt to quantify all of the costs because it did not believe that such costs would be incurred or were sizable enough to make a significant difference in the conclusions drawn from the analysis. However, EPA based part of its conclusion on a limited survey, of which the results had considerable uncertainty associated with the estimated cost of RRP work practices. We believe that new federal requirements to conduct retrospective analysis of existing rules, and existing requirements under the Regulatory Flexibility Act, provide opportunities to examine the implications of the use of Agency discretion and, where appropriate, make changes to achieve effective and fair federal rules.

Even where an effect may occur, it was not always possible to quantify it, as the necessary data were not available to make quantitative estimates for some effects. However, EPA did consider and address issues qualitatively where appropriate. For example, EPA's Economic Analysis qualitatively addressed the likely effects of the regulation on prices and social welfare. This is in accordance with Executive Order 12866 and EPA and OMB guidance, all of which acknowledge the role of qualitative information in economic analyses.

> **OIG Response 10:** The OIG acknowledges that it may not always be possible to quantify every effect of a rule, and that un-quantified effects are therefore qualified when appropriate. According to OMB guidance for Executive Order 12866, transfers such as insurance should not be included in the estimates of benefits and costs of a regulation. Instead, they should be addressed as part of the regulation's distributional effects (how both benefits and costs are distributed among subpopulations of particular concern). According to public comments for the Lead Rule and its amendment, renovators listed additional liability insurance as a cost firms would incur.

The Draft Report states that EPA did not estimate the costs to markets that are indirectly affected by the rule.

EPA disagrees that such estimates are appropriate. The Draft Report does not identify what markets other than the renovation, repair, and painting industry might be affected, or whether the magnitude (if any) of such costs justifies quantification. Moreover, EPA's Guidelines for Preparing Economic Analyses state that:

> "First, in most cases, the social costs of an environmental policy or other action can be measured with sufficient accuracy by limiting the analysis to the directly affected markets. This allows the analysis to focus on the sectors that must comply with a policy. In these cases, the disturbances that ripple outward from the directly affected markets to numerous other markets should have a minimal effect on the estimation of social costs. Second, a conventional partial equilibrium depiction and modeling of the directly affected markets will often be sufficient to measure social costs."

For this rule, the EPA concluded that the social costs can be measured with sufficient accuracy by limiting the modeling to the directly affected market. The professional judgment of EPA's staff was that the level and type of analysis it performed for the RRP rule was appropriate for the issues at hand.

Footnote 2: In discussing benefits analyses, the *Guidelines for Preparing Economic Analyses* provide the following implementation principles:
" Focus on key issues. Resources should be focused on benefit categories that are likely to influence policy decisions. To use time and resources effectively, analysts must weigh the costs of conducting additional analysis against the usefulness of the additional information provided for decision-making ... Additional data collection may not be warranted because it is unlikely to lead to significant changes in the conclusions of the analysis ... Likewise, some categories of benefits may not be assessed either because they are expected to be small or because the costs or time needed to quantify them far exceed the time or resource levels appropriate for analysis of the particular policy ... The *EA Guidelines* are designed to provide assistance to analysts in the economic analysis of environmental policies, but they do not provide a rigid blueprint or a "cookbook" for all policy assessments. The most productive and illuminating approaches for particular situations will depend on a variety of case-specific factors and will require professional judgment to apply."

OIG Response 11: As stated previously, we agree that the Agency can use its professional judgment, or discretion, in identifying what markets would be affected and the analyses it should perform as part of issuing a rule. However, EPA based part of its professional judgment on the results of a limited survey that had considerable uncertainty associated with the estimated cost of RRP work practices. EPA's initial determination that the costs of the Lead Rule were relatively low appears to have contributed to successive assumptions that other potential rule costs did not need to be considered. We believe new federal requirements to conduct retrospective analysis of existing rules, and existing requirements under the Regulatory Flexibility Act, provide opportunities to examine the implications of the use of Agency discretion and, where appropriate, make changes to achieve effective and fair federal rules. In the current regulatory environment, EPA can do more to assess the effectiveness of its discretionary rulemaking actions.

Additional Contractor Liability Insurance Costs Excluded From EPA's Analysis.

The Draft Report asserts that EPA's economic analysis is limited because it did not include contractors' liability insurance costs.

EPA disagrees. The RRP program reduces the renovation industry's potential liability because complying with the rule reduces exposure to lead dust and decreases the incidence of elevated blood levels. Because the RRP program reduces lead exposure from renovations and establishes a clear standard of care for renovation firms, it decreases liability for renovators. The RRP rule does not require contractors to purchase insurance. But the RRP rule can be expected to result in insurance becoming more readily available and less expensive for those renovators that voluntarily choose to purchase insurance coverage for lead pollution.

A 1994 General Accounting Office (GAO) report entitled "Lead Based Paint Hazards: Abatement Standards Are Needed to Ensure Availability of Insurance" (RCED-94- 231), written before EPA had published lead hazard standards or lead abatement regulations, concluded that the lack of lead abatement standards was one of the primary reasons that limited the availability of insurance for abatement firms. GAO concluded that lead abatement insurance would be easier to obtain and less expensive once EPA published standards for lead abatement. Similarly, EPA's RRP rule should make insurance more readily available and less expensive for those renovators who choose to purchase it.

OIG Response 12: The draft report states that in EPA's economic analysis, the Agency did not include the cost of contractors' additional liability insurance in the cost of complying with the Lead Rule.

Some of the public comments on the RRP Rule included renovation firms claiming that there would be increased costs for liability insurance. We recognize that the renovation firms are one of many viewpoints EPA receives as part of addressing public comments. Particularly because renovation firms are a directly affected market, EPA had the opportunity to evaluate whether there was any merit to the claim of increased costs for liability insurance.

-continued-

According to OMB guidance for Executive Order 12866, insurance should be addressed as part of the regulation's distributional effects. However, EPA did not address additional insurance costs in the analysis. Instead, as permitted by EPA's *2000 Guidelines for Preparing Economic Analyses*, the Agency used its discretion and decided not to analyze the potential impacts on liability insurance. With regard to the U.S. Government Accountability Office report, the referenced report is 18 years old and we do not believe it is relevant for insurance markets today. We continue to emphasize in our response that new federal requirements to conduct retrospective analysis of existing rules, and existing requirements under the Regulatory Flexibility Act, provide opportunities to examine the implications of the use of Agency discretion and, where appropriate, make changes to achieve effective and fair federal rules. In the current regulatory environment, EPA can do more to assess the effectiveness of its discretionary rulemaking actions.

Costs Associated With EPA Recommended Work Practices Excluded From EPA's Analysis

The Draft Report contends that excluding recommended work practices from the cost analysis is a limitation of that analysis.

EPA disagrees. Since the recommended work practices are not part of the rule, by definition they cannot affect the reliability of EPA's estimates of the rule's costs and benefits to society and are unrelated to the Economic Analysis. While OIG may believe that contractors may see little distinction between recommendations and requirements, not only is there no evidence to suggest it is true, accepted methodologies for regulatory analysis do not support estimating regulatory impacts from voluntary (recommended) activities. Moreover, the discussion in the OIG's draft report about EPA's authority to penalize firms may provide the mistaken impression that EPA can take action against firms that do not follow recommended work practices. However, EPA can only penalize renovation firms for failure to perform the required work practices described in the Code of Federal Regulations. EPA cannot take enforcement actions against firms that do not perform recommended work practices.

OIG Response 13: The OIG did not state in the draft report that there are costs for conducting recommended work practices that were not included in the cost estimate but should have been. Unfortunately, EPA appears to have misinterpreted the OIG's point of needing to clarify which work practices are required compared to the practices that are recommended. The OIG does not state that the costs associated with recommended work practices should have been included in the cost of complying with the Lead Rule. Rather, as stated in the draft report, we believe that the training manual needs clarification. When we were conducting our evaluation, EPA was recommending additional work practices in a mandatory training program on how to comply with the Lead Rule. The OIG maintains that contractors may believe that they could be liable for non-required, or recommended, work practices.

The Draft Report recommends that EPA include disclaimer language for the training course instructor manual, pertaining to EPA's economic analysis and impacts on individual contractors.

EPA agrees with the intent of this recommendation, but not the specific approach recommended. Instead of a disclaimer, EPA made several changes in the October 2011 instructor manual that further communicate the difference between required and recommended work practices. An Economic Analysis is not intended to serve as a cost estimation guide for individual members of the regulated community, either for actions that are required by regulation or for those that are merely recommended. Additionally, the primary purpose of the Lead Safety for Renovation, Repair and Painting training is to teach contractors about required work practices. Hence, the primary focus of the instructor manual is to provide Training Providers with material to communicate that required work practices must be performed to comply with the RRP regulations. As the result of changes made to the 2008 RRP rule, as noted above, EPA has already revised and published the updated instructor manual in October 2011.

Footnote 3: In the July 2010 issue of *Fine Homebuilding* magazine, the article titled "The EPA's new Renovation, Repair, and Painting Rule" contained the following question/response:
Q: Doesn't the RRP rule leave contractors vulnerable to potential lawsuits?
No. On the contrary, actually. If you've been working in older homes, you have already been assuming liability for the results of your remodeling work. (In other words, you could have been sued if your work endangered a child.) Adopting lead-safe work practices will reduce rather than increase the likelihood that your remodeling work will be linked to a case of lead poisoning, thereby lowering rather than increasing your liability. If you're certified and have documented the process properly, you're actually better protected from such suits.

> **OIG Response 14:** EPA agrees with the intent of recommendation 2. EPA's revisions to the training manual occurred after we notified the Agency of this issue. On September 1, 2011, the OIG provided EPA with preliminary report findings, which included a potential recommendation to add a disclaimer to the instructor manual to communicate the difference between required and recommended work practices. We acknowledge EPA's steps to improve the training manual and its communications on recommended versus required work practices.

Limitations in Benefit Analysis:

The Draft Report states that EPA acknowledged that it has limited confidence in the stated benefits because the Agency had not determined why the benefits analyses contained unusual results.

EPA believes the Draft Report fails to provide context for this statement. EPA stated in the preamble to the final rule (73 Federal Register 21751) that "EPA does not view the results as being sufficiently robust to represent the difference in magnitude of the benefits across regulatory alternatives. Nevertheless, EPA is confident that there are positive benefits."

> **OIG Response 15:** We agree and acknowledge that EPA believes there are positive benefits resulting from the final rule. Specifically, the draft report's first sentence in the section entitled *Limitations in Benefit Analysis* states: "In its economic analysis for the 2008 Lead Rule, EPA stated that the rule would generate substantial benefits."

The Draft Report points to EPA's sensitivity analysis indicating that variation in lead levels over time could decrease estimated benefits by 14 percent, and refers to statements made by the Clean Air Scientific Advisory Committee (CASAC) about the Dust Study.

EPA believes that the Draft Report failed to properly reference CASAC's finding, particularly that uncertainty can also lead to underestimating benefits. CASAC concluded that these factors, as well as others "might lead to either an overestimate or an underestimate of risk, and hence an overestimate or underestimate of the benefits of the regulation." CASAC did not conclude solely that benefits were overestimated. CASAC stated elsewhere in the report that it was concerned that OPPT's methodology was likely to underestimate IQ loss. One of CASAC's overarching concerns was that EPA should give greater priority to decreasing childhood lead exposures. CASAC stated that there is ample evidence that exposure of children to lead dust poses a major health risk, and it concluded that renovation and repair activities where lead-based paint surfaces are present requires practices that minimize dust exposure to children. CASAC suggested adopting more stringent practices than EPA proposed in order to better protect children from lead dust. These are indications that CASAC felt the benefits of controlling lead dust from renovation exceeds the cost, whatever the specific magnitude of the benefits and costs.

> **OIG Response 16:** We agree that CASAC discussed positive aspects of EPA's plan to analyze the Lead Rule. For example, the OIG draft report states that CASAC found that the dust study was reasonably well designed considering the complexity of the problem, and that the report provided information not available from any other source. However, CASAC also identified some key limitations in the analysis that were used to determine the benefits. For example, the dust study was most likely not statistically valid or nationally representative because of the limited data used. Also, CASAC found that the data were inadequate to support the proposed modeling approach for estimating the IQ changes in children exposed during renovations.

OIG asserts that the effect of the structures' age in the Dust Study on the benefits estimates is a significant limitation that provides a rationale for reconsidering the requirements of the RRP rule.

EPA disagrees. While most of the housing used in the Dust Study was built prior to 1930, the distribution of paint lead levels on components worked on covered a broad range from 0.8% to 10.2% lead by weight for interior jobs and from 1.3% to 16.8% lead by weight for exterior jobs. These ranges of paint lead levels are consistent with the range of levels reported in the National Survey of Lead and Allergens in Housing for components with lead-based paint. Thus, the range of structures in the Dust Study did provide a reasonable basis for EPA's analysis.

Furthermore, EPA's charge questions specifically requested CASAC's advice on how to adjust the estimates based on changes in lead levels in paint over time. The CASAC Panel did not recommend a suggested approach for making such an adjustment. Because there were significant uncertainties in how to accurately adjust benefits for variations in lead levels over time, it was appropriate for EPA to address the adjustment in the sensitivity analysis. Since EPA's primary estimate was that benefits were 69 percent to 313 percent larger than the costs, net benefits would still be positive and substantial even if benefits decreased by 14 percent due to an adjustment for change in lead levels over time.

OIG Response 17: The OIG did not assert that the effect of the structures' age in the dust study provides a rationale for reconsidering the requirements of the RRP rule. The OIG also did not state that the structures' age was a <u>significant</u> limitation, but does acknowledge that it is a limitation nonetheless. EPA also acknowledges that the structures' age is a limitation as it states above, "The CASAC Panel did not recommend a suggested approach for making such an adjustment. Because there were significant uncertainties in how to accurately adjust benefits for variations in lead levels over time, it was appropriate for EPA to address the adjustment in the sensitivity analysis."

Conclusions

OIG's report states that EPA went forward with the rule because its benefit-cost analysis indicated that the rule generated substantial benefits.

EPA went forward with the rule because it was required to do so by statute. Work practices were necessary to address lead-based paint hazards and were based (as directed by the statutory standard) on studies of renovation activities. Based on the results of the four-phase study entitled "Lead Exposure Associated with Renovation and Remodeling Activities," EPA concluded that all renovations that disturb lead-based paint create lead-based paint hazards. Upon making this finding, EPA was obligated to issue regulations under TSCA § 402(c)(3) that addressed those hazards, taking into account reliability, effectiveness, and safety. EPA reviewed a number of studies in developing work practice requirements, but the Characterization of Dust Lead Levels After Renovation, Repair, and Painting Activities (the "Dust Study") was EPA's primary work practice resource in crafting the requirements of the final RRP rule.

OIG Response 18: We agree that our draft report states that EPA went forward with the rule because its benefit-cost analysis indicated that the rule generated substantial benefits. However, that is not a complete representation of the OIG's position. For example, the OIG also recognizes that EPA was required to do so by statute. The OIG also does not question the dust study as being the most useful data available at the time EPA was issuing the Lead Rule. Although the dust study may have been the best available information, there were limitations with the data that were acknowledged by not only CASAC but also by EPA. As the OIG has represented throughout its response, we acknowledge that EPA was under time pressures and a mandate to issue the Lead Rule. Even under optimal conditions, federal agencies may not have access to the quality information needed to conduct sufficient economic and benefits analysis for federal rulemaking purposes. The constraints EPA was operating under were factors in the quality and quantity of information it relied on in developing the economic and benefits analysis for the Lead Rule. However, in the current regulatory environment, EPA has other options than to solely rely on decisions and analyses that were admittedly developed under less than optimal rulemaking conditions. We believe that the new federal requirements to conduct retrospective analysis of existing rules, as well as the existing requirements under the Regulatory Flexibility Act, provide opportunities to examine the implications of the use of Agency discretion and, where appropriate, make changes to achieve effective and fair federal rules.

Distribution

Office of the Administrator
Assistant Administrator for Chemical Safety and Pollution Prevention
Agency Follow-Up Official (the CFO)
Agency Follow-Up Coordinator
General Counsel
Associate Administrator for Congressional and Intergovernmental Relations
Associate Administrator for External Affairs and Environmental Education
Audit Follow-Up Coordinator, Office of Chemical Safety and Pollution Prevention